WEIRD WEATHER

STRANGE SKIES

JOANNE MATTERN

Enslow PUBLISHING

Please visit our website, www.enslow.com. For a free color catalog of all our high-quality books,
call toll free 1-800-398-2504 or fax 1-877-980-4454

Published in 2027 by
Enslow Publishing
2544 Clinton Street
Buffalo, NY 14224

Cataloging-in-Publication Data
Names: Mattern, Joanne, 1963-.
Title: Strange skies / Joanne Mattern.
Description: Buffalo, NY : Enslow Publishing, 2027. | Series: Weird weather | Includes glossary.
Identifiers: ISBN 9781978549784 (pbk.) | ISBN 9781978549791 (library bound) | ISBN 9781978549807 (ebook)
Subjects: LCSH: Meteorological optics--Juvenile literature. | Astronomy--Juvenile literature. | Rainbows--Juvenile literature. | Sky--Juvenile literature.
Classification: LCC QC975.3 M375 2027 | DDC 551.565--dc23

Photos Credits: Cover, p.1 ©2024 Sibsamshota/Shutterstock.com; p.3 and throughout the book ©2020 Cherisha Kay Norman/Shutterstock.com; p.4, p.29 ©2019 Photoflying/Shutterstock.com; p.5 ©2024 AstroStar/Shutterstock.com; p.6 ©2019 detchana wangkheeree (cloud background spiral was added)/Shutterstock.com; p.6, p.7 ©2018 Alexandra Lande/Shutterstock.com; p.8, p.29 ©2017 Simon's passion 4 Travel/Shutterstock.com; p.9 ©2022 Abstract51/Shutterstock.com; p.10, p.11 ©2024 John D Sirlin/Shutterstock.com; p.12 ©2025 muratart/Shutterstock.com; p.13, p.29 ©2019 Artsiom P/Shutterstock.com; p.14, p.28 ©2024 Oguzhan Daldaban/Shutterstock.com; p.15 ©2017 OKSANA FERKHOVA/Shutterstock.com; p.16, p.17 ©2024 photomalin/Shutterstock.com; p.18, p.28 ©2025 skywings00/Shutterstock.com; p.19 ©2015 opportunity_2015/Shutterstock.com; p.20, p.21 ©2015 Digital signal/Shutterstock.com; p.22 ©2018 aaltair/Shutterstock.com; p.23 ©2020 Uwe Michael Neumann/Shutterstock.com; p.24 public domain/National Observatory of Japan; p.25 ©2009 Andre Nantel/Shutterstock.com; p.26 ©2021 Icemeadow Studios/Shutterstock.com; p.26, p.27 ©2017 John D Sirlin/Shutterstock.com

Printed in China

CPSIA compliance information: Batch #QSENS27: For further information, contact Enslow Publishing, New York, New York, at 1-800-398-2504.

TABLE OF CONTENTS

Words in the glossary appear in **bold** type the first time they are used in the text.

SPIRALS IN THE SKY

It was a hot August night in 2025. Thousands of people had their eyes to the sky. It was time for the annual Perseid meteor shower. Every year, meteors flash across the sky. It's a dazzling display of light.

But this time, some people got an extra treat. Strange light spirals appeared over Maryland, New York, and several other states. Soon, photos and videos of the strange lights were all over social media.

Scientists studied the videos. They quickly figured out what happened. Shortly before the spirals appeared, a rocket had taken off from South America. As the upper part of the rocket was ejected, it tumbled through the air. The spirals came from sunlight hitting the frozen **exhaust** given off by the rocket.

The strange skies on that August night were caused by rockets. But some strange skies are natural **phenomena**. Let's look at some of the strangest things you might see in the sky.

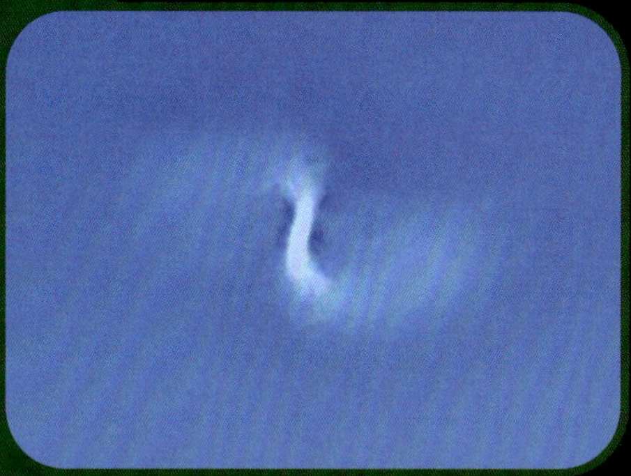

ROCKET EXHAUST SPIRAL

STAYING IN SHAPE

*Why was the spiral shape so clear? One scientist explained that because the spiral was in space, there was no air to **distort** it.*

LIGHT IT UP

If you live in the far northern parts of the world, you may be lucky enough to see the aurora borealis. It is also called the northern lights.

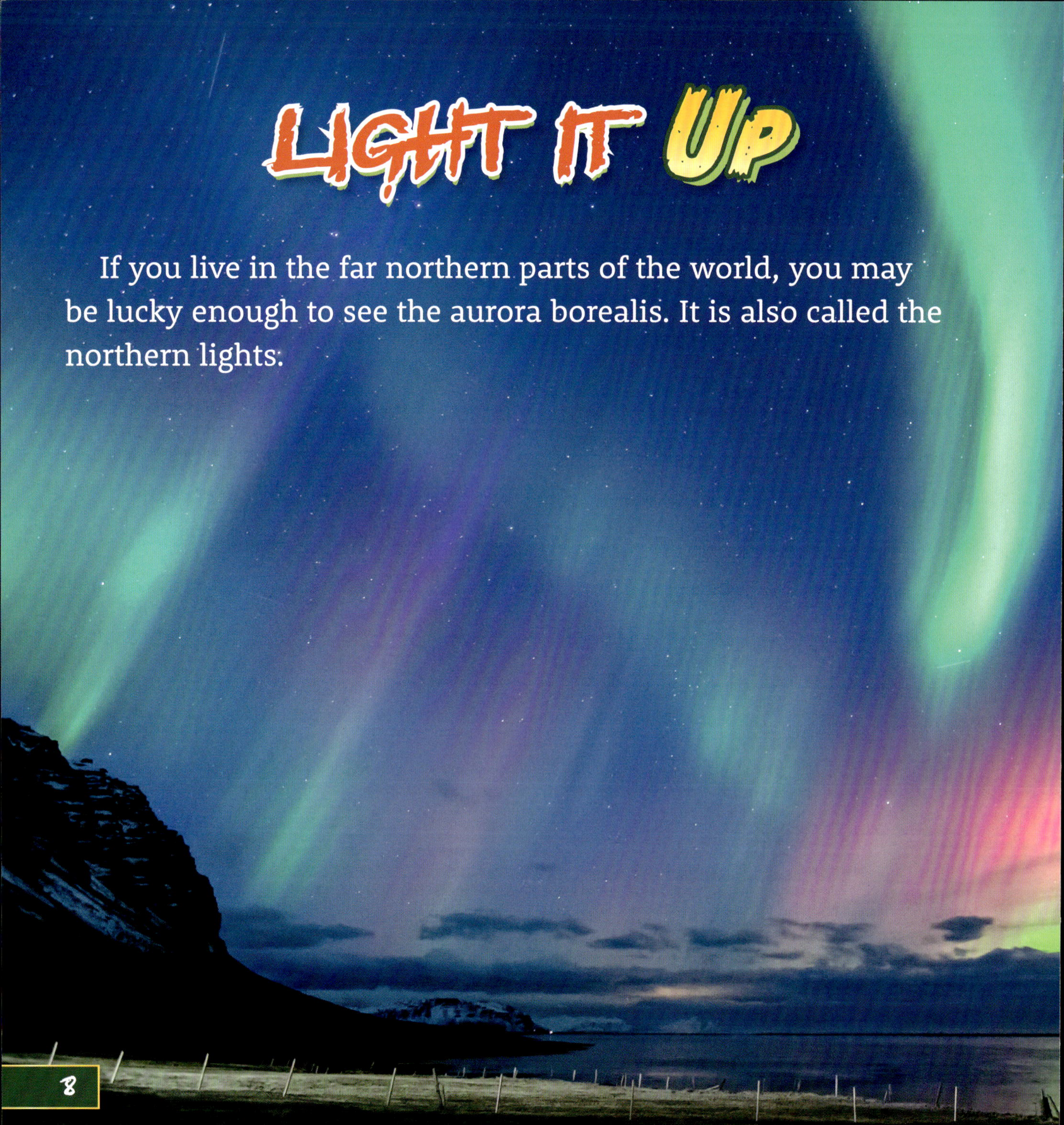

Auroras form when **solar** wind hits Earth's **atmosphere**. Solar wind is made up of **charged** particles from the Sun. These are called protons and neutrons. When they reach the atmosphere, they are pulled toward the North and South Poles by magnetic charges. The particles mix with gases in the atmosphere. This mixture causes them to light up the sky.

COLORFUL LIGHTS

Different gases in the atmosphere create different colors. The northern lights can be red, green, pink, blue, and purple.

The closer you are to the North Pole, the better chance you have of seeing the northern lights. Alaska, Iceland, and Norway are some of the best places.

However, sometimes these lights can be seen farther south. During the summer of 2025, the lights could be seen as far south as Arizona and New Mexico!

SOUTHERN LIGHTS

Auroras appear near the South Pole too. Here, they are called aurora australis, or the southern lights.

STORMY SUN

We mentioned solar wind. But did you know that there are solar storms too?

Solar storms happen when energy and magnetic particles explode from the Sun's surface. These explosions send clouds of energy toward Earth. These clouds can't be seen with the naked eye. But they do cause an amazing aurora borealis.

Solar storms can affect life on Earth. These giant bursts of energy can block radio broadcasts. They can mess up wireless signals. They can even cause power outages.

A SCARY DAY

On September 1, 1859, a powerful solar storm called the Carrington Event struck Earth. The storm created electrical currents that were so strong, they shocked people and started fires.

TRIPLE SUNS

What's better than one Sun? How about three? An event called a sundog creates a bright spot of light on either side of the Sun. It looks like three suns hanging in the sky!

Sundogs happen when sunlight is bent by ice crystals in the atmosphere. They usually happen in very cold weather, when there are more ice crystals. The ice acts like a **prism**. It reflects the light.

Sometimes sundogs look a little like rainbows. They glow red on the side near the Sun. They glow blue on the far side.

BY ANY OTHER NAME

Sundogs are also called "mock suns" or "parhelia." That word means "with the Sun."

Can sundogs predict the weather? Some people think so. They say if you see a sundog, it will rain in the next 24 hours.

Sometimes, moondogs appear in the night sky. Like sundogs, a moondog can show up when moonlight reflects off light crystals in the sky. These only happen when the Moon is full and low in the sky. And like sundogs, some people say that a moondog or a **halo** around the Moon means rain or snow will fall the next day.

TOWERS AND CIRCLES

Light can do funny things in the atmosphere. Sometimes, long towers of light appear in a line above or below the Sun or the Moon. These towers are called light pillars. Like other sky lights, these happen when sunlight shines on ice crystals in the atmosphere.

Strange lights can be seen in other patterns too. Sometimes the wind can move ice crystals around. When the sunlight strikes the crystals, they can appear as lines or circles.

STREETLIGHT MAGIC

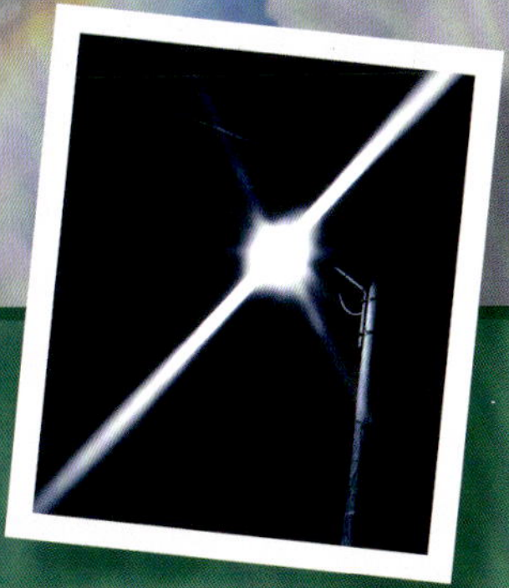

Light pillars can also appear around streetlights!

Another type of sun pillar is called a crepuscular ray. That name might sound scary. But these rays are harmless! They happen when the Sun is low in the sky or hidden behind clouds. Some rays of sun peek through the clouds, sending long streaks toward the ground.

Where do crepuscular rays get their creepy name? The word *crepuscular* means "dim" or "twilight." These rays usually appear when the sky is getting dark.

DIRTY SKIES

Dust, smoke, or drops of water in the air help us see crepuscular rays.

RARE RAINBOWS

You've probably seen a rainbow in the sky after a storm. Rainbows form when sunlight reflects off water in the sky. The water acts like a prism. It breaks the light rays into separate colors.

Sometimes, an entire cloud can hold a rainbow. But it has to be very cold for that to happen. Rainbow clouds form in the second layer of Earth's atmosphere. Temperatures there can be –130 degrees Fahrenheit (–90 degrees Celsius)! As the Sun's light scatters through ice crystals in the air, it breaks apart and forms a rainbow.

THE HAND OF HUMANS

Not all strange skies are caused by natural events. Many are caused by people. We already talked about the strange spirals that appeared when light hit frozen exhaust coming from a rocket. But many more strange sky events have occurred.

THE SUBARU TELESCOPE ATOP THE MAUNA KEA VOLCANO IN HAWAII

In 2023, a camera on a mountain in Hawaii recorded green lines hanging in the sky. The lights looked like something from a video game. Scientists said they came from lasers fired toward Earth from a spacecraft high in the sky.

A company called SpaceX has fired many rockets. Sometimes, these cause strange lights and colors. Many people have seen Starlink satellites. These satellites look like boxes of light moving across the night.

In July 2023, people in the western United States saw a blood-red streak in the sky. It was caused when a SpaceX rocket punched a hole in the atmosphere. The rocket's carbon dioxide and water **vapor** combined with oxygen atoms to create a red glow. As we send more crafts into space, the sight of strange skies will become even more common!

ROCKET GOING INTO SPACE

SPACEX ROCKET OVER PHOENIX, ARIZONA

WHAT AM I?

Can you guess what type of strange skies are shown in each photo? Look closely at these images and use the clues to help you figure it out. Then, check your answers below. How many did you get right?

1

I rise from the Sun like a tower of light. What am I?

2

There's just one Sun, but there are three of me! What am I?

3

Big storms on the Sun make the night sky bright with color. What am I?

4

Look up at the night sky and you might see my lights streaking past. What am I?

5

My flares and fountains of fire can interfere with life on Earth. What am I?

1. light pillar; 2. sundog; 3. aurora borealis; 4. Perseid meteor shower; 5. solar storm

GLOSSARY

atmosphere (AT-muhs-feer): the mixture of gases that surrounds Earth

charged (CHAHRJD): having electrical energy

distort (di-STORT): to twist out of the normal shape

exhaust (ig-ZAWST): the gases given off by an engine

halo (HAY-loh): a ring of light around an object

phenomena (feh-NOM-eh-nuh): an interesting event that you can see

prism (PRIZ-uhm): a clear, solid glass shape that breaks up light into the colors of the spectrum

solar (SOH-lur): having to do with the Sun

vapor (VAY-pur): a gas formed from something that is usually a liquid or solid at normal temperatures

FACT CHECK

1. The aurora borealis can be seen ___________.
   a. only in the north   b. only in the south   c. in both the north and south
2. Solar storms can block ___________.
   a. sunlight   b. radio waves   c. auroras
3. People's activities have caused ___________ strange skies.
   a. more   b. fewer   c. no

Answers: 1. a, 2. b, 3. a

FURTHER READING

Betts, Bruce. *The Sun: Our Solar System's Star.* Lerner Publications, 2025.

Bullard, Lisa. *Auroras.* The Child's World, Inc., 2025.

McDonald, Jill. *Rockets and Other Space Machines.* Doubleday Books for Young Readers, 2025.

ON THE INTERNET

Sun
https://kids.britannica.com/students/article/Sun/276056
This Britannica Kids article explains the Sun and different kinds of solar activity.

Curious Kids: What Causes the Northern Lights?
https://theconversation.com/curious-kids-what-causes-the-northern-lights-111573
Discover what causes the northern lights and why they are different colors.

Publisher's note to educators and parents: Our editors have carefully reviewed these websites to ensure that they are suitable for students. Many websites change frequently, however, and we cannot guarantee that a site's future contents will continue to meet our high standards of quality and educational value. Be advised that students should be closely supervised whenever they access the internet.

INDEX

ABOUT THE AUTHOR

Joanne Mattern is the author of many books for children on a variety of subjects, including science, history, and biography. She loves writing about and experiencing weird weather events! Joanne loves to learn about people, places, and events and bring historical figures to life for today's readers. She lives in New York State with her family.